GAME DAY
TEXAS FOOTBALL

GAME DAY
TEXAS FOOTBALL

The Greatest Games, Players, Coaches and Teams
in the Glorious Tradition of Longhorn Football

TRIUMPH
B O O K S
CHICAGO

Athlon® Sports™
AMERICA'S PREMIER SPORTS ANNUALS

Library of Congress Control Number: 2005930365

This book is available in quantity at special discounts for your group or organization.
For further information, contact:

Triumph Books
542 South Dearborn Street
Suite 750
Chicago, Illinois 60605
(312) 939-3330
Fax (312) 663-3557

EDITORS: Rob Doster, Kevin Daniels

PHOTO EDITOR: Tim Clark

DESIGN: Anderson Thomas Design

PHOTO CREDITS: Athlon Sports Archive; University of Texas Sports Information; AP/Wide World

Printed in U.S.A.
ISBN-13: 978-1-57243-760-9
ISBN-10: 1-57243-760-X

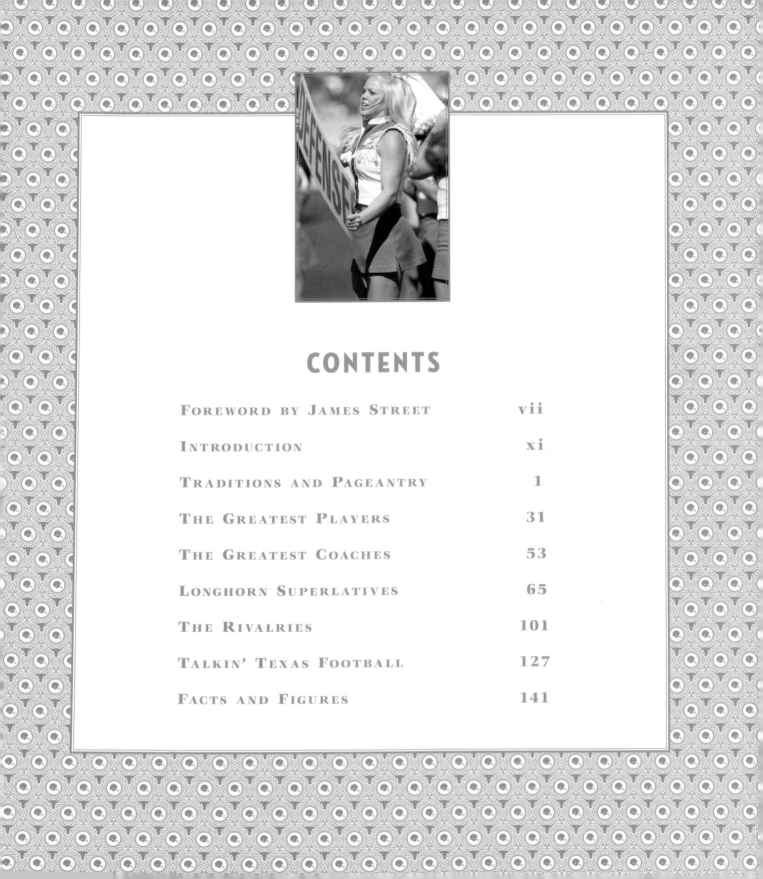

CONTENTS

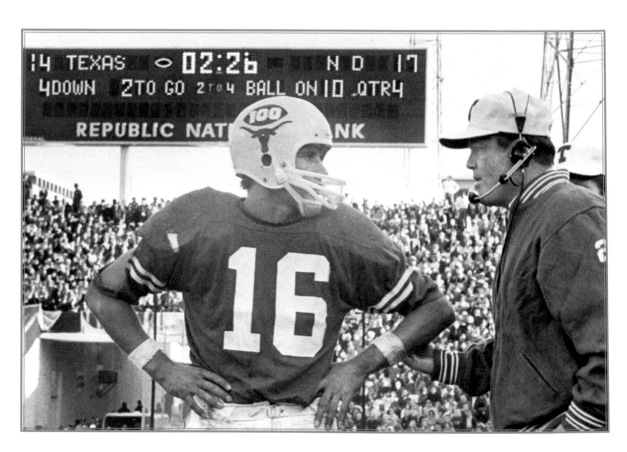

One of the great moments in Texas football. The scoreboard tells the story, as James Street confers with Darrell K. Royal on UT's game-winning drive in the 1970 Cotton Bowl victory over No. 9 Notre Dame. Street hit Cotton Speyrer for an eight-yard gain on the critical fourth-down play.

Foreword

I was watching the national champion Longhorn baseball team play recently when it occurred to me what a special fraternity the Texas Longhorn football program is. Coach Darrell Royal was at the baseball game, and everyone in the stands was interested in talking to him, even though he retired in 1976. There's a lot of pride in saying that I played for such a great coach and for a school like Texas, and it's a pride that all Longhorn fans share.

All the athletes who were associated with Coach Royal at the time were living a dream, and it was a great opportunity. It's important that today's players understand how important it is to be a Longhorn and to make the most of it.

One of the greatest moves Coach Mack Brown made was to reunite the members of the football family who have played for the University of Texas. He brought back the tradition, which has always been there but had waned a little bit. That has helped build on the foundation and has made the family stronger. Being a Longhorn causes a feeling of pride unlike any other.

Some of my greatest memories as a Longhorn include the opportunity to play in the Texas-Arkansas games and against Notre Dame in the 1970 Cotton Bowl. Notre Dame was coming out of retirement, so to speak, to play in the bowl game (the Irish hadn't played in a bowl since 1925), and their name was synonymous with college football back

then. They were the only team you could watch on Sundays; the Fighting Irish's games were replayed on that day. So it was especially meaningful to win that game 21–17 in a thrilling comeback and complete an unbeaten National Championship season.

I have great memories of my time at Texas, but what's especially amazing to me is the fact that, more than three decades later, so many people remember the things our team accomplished during my time as a Longhorn. It was just a neat experience. As I have gotten older, I realize just how lucky I was and how everything fell into place for me. I got to meet President Nixon after the Arkansas game in 1969 and President Johnson after the Notre Dame game that year. Later on, I went to Las Vegas and had the fortune to meet Elvis backstage and Bill

Medley of the Righteous Brothers. (Elvis said Texas deserved to beat Arkansas, while Bill Medley said he wanted Arkansas to win. I always was an Elvis fan!)

There is a lot of pride when you become a Longhorn. When you come to UT, you have access to a network of people for the rest of your life, whether you were a starter or not. When you go out to the business world, being a Longhorn means a lot. People always want to talk about my playing days and what's going on these days. My time at Texas opened several doors for me, and it continues to do so 30 years later.

I look back, and it all seems like it was a fairy tale or someone else's life. I'm thankful for the memories and everything UT has done for me.

—JAMES STREET

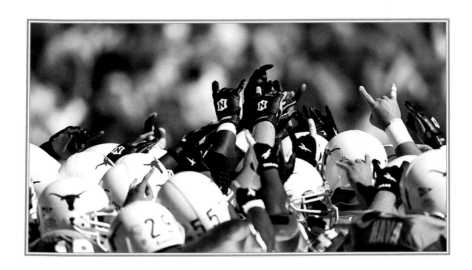

Introduction

The images are unforgettable and too numerous to count.

Thousands of hands thrust skyward with the familiar "Hook 'em Horns" sign welcoming their burnt orange-clad Longhorns. Big Bertha and the Showband of the Southwest pounding out another rendition of "The Eyes of Texas." Earl Campbell and Ricky Williams running to Heisman glory. The epic 15–14 win over Arkansas that gave Texas the 1969 national title. Darrell Royal prowling the sidelines as his teams dominated the Southwest Conference. Memorable tilts with rivals Oklahoma and Texas A&M.

We're distilling the pageantry and drama of Texas football into the pages that follow. It's a daunting task. Few college football programs in the country inspire the loyalty and passion that Texas football exacts from its fans—and with good reason.

Through the words and images we present, you'll get a taste of what Texas football is all about. Decades have passed since players first donned the burnt orange, but one thing hasn't changed: Longhorn football is a tradition, a legacy of greatness, a virtual way of life in the Lone Star State.

TRADITIONS AND PAGEANTRY

The sights and sounds of Game Day in Austin create an unmatched spectacle, a glorious mix of tradition and color and pomp and pageantry. Here's a small sample of what makes Texas football unique.

The Colors and Nickname

They're as familiar to Texas fans as the Lone Star on the state flag—the Longhorns, clad in burnt orange and white.

The University of Texas began playing football in 1893 with gold and white as its colors, and the nickname of "Varsity." In 1900, the University's Board of Regents officially declared the school's colors to be orange and white. Three years later, Daily Texan sportswriter D. A. Frank referred to the team as Longhorns. After years of continuous usage, the unofficial moniker became the team's official nickname.

Bevo

The University of Texas students were presented with a Longhorn steer at halftime of the 1916 Texas A&M game by a group led by Stephen Pinckney, a UT alum and official with the U.S. Attorney General's office. Ever since then, the lean, tenacious animal has been the school's mascot. There are conflicting accounts regarding the origin of his name, including one that involves a non-alcoholic near beer named Bevo that was on the market at that time. Another version has some Aggies kidnapping the steer after their loss to Texas in 1916 and branding it with the 13–0 score of the 1915 game, which A&M had won. Upon the animal's return, some enterprising Texas students changed the 13 to a B, the dash to an E, inserted a V and left the O as it was—BEVO. The most likely explanation is that Bevo is a play on the word "beeve," a slang term that means "steer" and was in common usage in the Southwest in the early decades of the 20th century. By the way, Texas won that 1916 Texas A&M contest with the Aggies 21–7.

Hook 'em Horns

Texas cheerleader Harley Clark instituted the Hook 'em Horns hand signal at a pep rally preceding the 1955 TCU game. Henry Pitts, a University of Texas student, was the one who actually came up with the gesture, symbolizing Longhorn mascot Bevo's horns, as a shadow-casting idea. Pitts shared his inspiration with Clark, and at the game against the Horned Frogs on Saturday, Texas lost 40–27 but saw the birth of an institution, as the Hook 'em Horns signal surged repeatedly from one end of the stadium to the other.

The Spring Jamboree

At the instigation of coach Mack Brown, the annual spring scrimmage has been expanded into a weekend event that draws former lettermen and their families to campus for a reunion, a golf outing and an autograph session. Of course, the Orange-White scrimmage still takes center stage. Since the inaugural Jamboree in 1998, attendance has skyrocketed each year. In 2004, 36,250 Longhorn faithful turned out for the extravaganza.

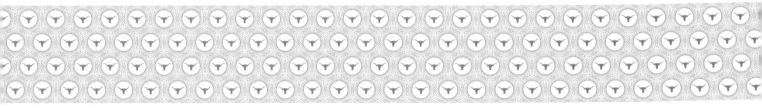

The Showband of the Southwest

The University of Texas marching band was founded in 1900, before the football team was called the Longhorns and the same year the Board of Regents declared the school colors to be orange and white. Chemistry professor Dr. E. P. Schoch, in an effort to drum up campus-wide interest in the football team, raised $150 to purchase instruments from Jackson's Pawn Shop in Austin and collected a group of 16 musicians to add to the excitement at Clark Field on fall Saturdays. From those humble beginnings, what later became known as the Showband of the Southwest was born.

Dr. H. E. Baxter was the band's first director and served in that capacity for five years. Under the directorship of Colonel George E. Hurt from 1937 to 1949, the band grew to over 200 members. The band currently encompasses 360 members, and although it requires a year-round commitment as a course offered by the School of Music, many different academic disciplines are represented.

As pregame excitement builds to a fever pitch in Royal-Memorial Stadium, the stands bulging with over 80,000 spectators, the band explodes out of the tunnel in perfect formation, following the world's largest bass drum—Big Bertha—onto the field, all hands raised in the "hook 'em" sign. The Longhorn band then plays "Deep in the Heart of Texas" and covers half the field with a giant block-T as 900 pounds and 777 square yards of Texas state flag are unfurled over the other half of the field. The football team then enters the playing field through the T.

The Showband of the Southwest has marched at presidential inauguration parades, inspiring a "hook 'em" sign from President George W. Bush in 2001. In 1986, it was awarded the Sudler Trophy, recognizing the top university marching band in the nation. Many of the band members also participate in one or more of three concert bands: two jazz ensembles and a basketball-game pep band.

Big Bertha

The largest bass drum in the world—Big Bertha—belongs to the University of Texas' marching band. Although she has been a staple of the Longhorn band performances since 1955, Big Bertha is actually more than 80 years old. She was actually built for the University of Chicago and was first used in the Chicago-Princeton game in 1922. After a period of inactivity subsequent to the Maroons' discontinuing their football program, Colonel D. Harold Byrd purchased Bertha for the Longhorn Band.

Big Bertha is eight feet in diameter and 54 inches wide, and when mounted on her trailer, she stands over 10 feet tall. Prior to each game in Royal-Memorial Stadium, a group of students known as the "Bertha Crew" rolls the giant drum onto the field ahead of the Showband of the Southwest, and the stadium crowd erupts. During games Big Bertha is stationed in the end zone, where she greets every Longhorn score with loud booming while being spun around by the crew.

The UT Tower

The 27-story UT Tower serves not only as the Main Building on the Austin campus, but it also heralds the football team's great triumphs. For all regular-season victories other than Texas A&M, and all non-BCS bowl wins, the building is lit orange on top with a white shaft. For wins over Texas A&M, and Big 12 Conference and South Division titles, the tower is lit up entirely in orange. A Longhorns national championship finds an all-orange lighting with a "#1" display.

— Torchlight Parade for the Texas-Oklahoma Game —

The first Torchlight Parade and Rally took place the day before Thanksgiving in 1916 to support the team as it prepared to play Texas A&M. Today, the Red River Shootout is the object of the event. The leaders of various campus spirit organizations carry torches while leading the Longhorn band and student body around campus on foot. The parade begins at the northwest corner of campus and winds around a predetermined route until it reaches the Main Mall. An elaborate pep rally ensues there, complete with the Longhorn band, Smokey the cannon, Bevo, performances by the cheerleaders and the draping of a huge Texas flag over the Main Building, giving the football team a Texas-sized sendoff to Dallas.

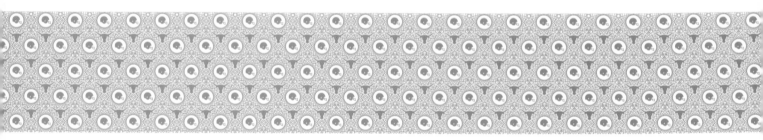

Darrell K Royal-Texas Memorial Stadium

In the days leading up to the Thanksgiving Day, 1923, game with Texas A&M, Texas athletic director Theo Bellmont began openly campaigning for a concrete stadium to replace Clark Field as a home football venue. Plans were drawn up and the facility was completed in record time. The stadium, with a seating capacity of 27,000, was dedicated on Thanksgiving Day, 1924, with the Longhorns defeating the Aggies 7–0. The student body, which had been instrumental along with Bellmont in turning the stadium from an idea to a reality, decided it must be dedicated to the veterans from the state of Texas who had fought in World War I.

In 1926 the north end was closed in, creating a horseshoe and increasing seating capacity to 40,500. Subsequent expansions have brought the stands to their current capacity of 80,082. For 27 years, beginning in 1969, the playing surface was AstroTurf, until it was removed following the 1995 season and replaced with Prescription Athletic Turf. The PAT in turn was replaced in 2002 with Bermudagrass.

In 1996 the stadium was rededicated to honor the memory of all American war veterans. Also that year, the name of Darrell K. Royal, the coach who brought three national titles to the University of Texas, was added to that of the stadium.

"The Eyes of Texas"

The eyes of Texas are upon you

all the live long day....

The eyes of Texas are upon you,

you cannot get away....

Do not think you can escape them

at night or early in the morn....

The eyes of Texas are upon you

'til Gabriel blows his horn.

"Texas Fight"

Texas Fight, Texas Fight,

And it's goodbye to A&M.

Texas Fight, Texas Fight,

And we'll put over one more win.

Texas Fight, Texas Fight,

For it's Texas that we love the best.

Give 'em hell! Give 'em hell!

Go Horns, Go!

And it's goodbye to all the rest.

(YELL)

Yea Orange! Yea White!

Yea Longhorns! Fight! Fight! Fight!

Texas Fight! Texas Fight!

Yea Texas Fight!

Texas Fight! Texas Fight!

Yea Texas Fight!

(repeat chorus)

THE GREATEST PLAYERS

Texas' roster of greats reads like a who's who of college football legends. The names are familiar to fans of college football, and for the fans of Texas' rivals, they still bring a shiver of dread. Here are some of the stars who have shone brightest during their tenures in Austin.

SCOTT APPLETON
Tackle, 1961-63

As a senior in 1963, Appleton finished fifth in Heisman Trophy voting. Not bad for a tackle. He was a key performer on three of the best Longhorn teams of all time, a leader of the '63 national champions and was the only consensus All-American on its roster.

HUB BECHTOL
End, 1944-46

Bechtol played end for coach Dana X. Bible's last three Longhorn teams. A three-time All-American and the first consensus All-American in Texas history, he was also one of the greatest receivers to wear the burnt orange and white. During his time in Austin, he was the receiving end of a combo that found another Hall of Famer—Bobby Layne—on the passing end.

CEDRIC BENSON
Running Back, 2001-04

In 2004, Benson passed Earl Campbell into second place on UT's career rushing list with 5,540 yards, second only to Ricky Williams' 6,279. Benson's 64 career rushing touchdowns are also second-most in school history. He ran for over 1,000 yards all four years of his college career—1,053 as a freshman, 1,293 as a sophomore, 1,306 as a junior, and 1,834 (third on the UT single-season charts) as a senior. Also as a senior, he captured the Doak Walker Award as the nation's best running back.

EARL CAMPBELL
Tailback, 1974-77

As a freshman, Campbell ran for 928 yards playing fullback in coach Darrell Royal's wishbone offense. Fred Akers replaced Royal as coach in 1977 and made Campbell the deep back in the I formation. Campbell became Texas' first Heisman Trophy winner that year, when he rushed for 1,744 yards (a Southwest Conference record that stood for 16 years) and 19 touchdowns. He led the nation in rushing and scoring that fall and set a UT record with 10 100-yard games. Campbell is a member of both the College and Pro Football Halls of Fame.

"Earl Campbell is the greatest football player I have ever seen, and Ann Campbell (Earl's mother and inspiration) is the best coach there ever was!" TEXAS COACH FRED AKERS, AFTER CAMPBELL'S 173-YARD PERFORMANCE AGAINST HOUSTON DESPITE SUFFERING FROM THE FLU

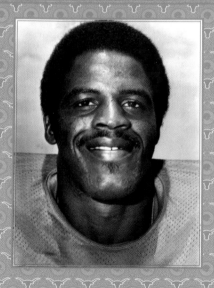

"I will represent what a Heisman Trophy winner should be.
Thank you very much." CAMPBELL, UPON RECEIVING THE HEISMAN

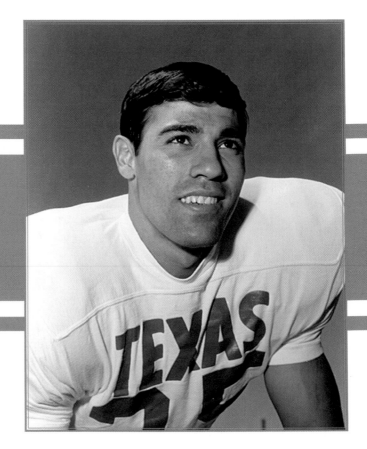

CHRIS GILBERT
Running Back, 1966-68

Gilbert was the first player in NCAA history to rush for 1,000 yards in each season he was eligible (at that time, freshmen were not eligible). As a sophomore, Gilbert ran for 1,080 yards, and he finished his career with 3,321 yards—both were UT records at the time. As a junior in 1967, he recorded the longest run from scrimmage in Longhorn history with a 96-yard touchdown jaunt against TCU. He concluded his career in 1968, the year the wishbone attack was unleashed on the nation, and ran for 1,132 yards at 6.2 per carry, with 13 touchdowns. He still ranks fourth on Texas' career rushing chart.

DERRICK JOHNSON
Linebacker, 2001-04

If Johnson isn't the greatest linebacker in Texas football history, he certainly ranks right up there with Tommy Nobis. Johnson was big, fast, explosive and instinctive. In 2001 he was national Freshman of the Year. He was consensus first-team All-Big 12 each of the next three years and consensus first-team All-America as a junior and senior. In 2004 he won the Butkus Award as the nation's best linebacker and the Nagurski Award as the nation's best defensive player. Over his career he recorded 458 total tackles, 65 tackles for loss, 30 pass breakups and nine interceptions.

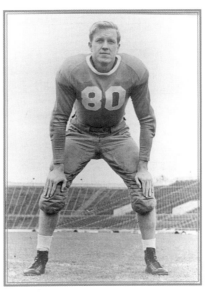

MALCOLM KUTNER
End, 1939-41

In 1941, Coach Dana X. Bible's Texas team was one of the best in the nation, and Kutner was its most decorated player. He was a three-sport star at UT, earning three letters in football, three in basketball and one in track. In football, Kutner's primary position was end, but versatility was his forte. He was perfectly suited for Bible's balanced, innovative offense, leading the Longhorns to an 8–1–1 record and a fourth-place national ranking. As a pro with the Chicago Cardinals, Kutner was a three-year All-Pro and league MVP in 1948.

BOBBY LAYNE
Quarterback, 1944-47

Layne is generally regarded as not only one of the greatest quarterbacks in Texas history, but also one of the greatest of all time. He entered the university on scholarship to play baseball— he was an accomplished pitcher—but it wasn't long before coach Dana X. Bible recruited him to throw the football as well. He completed 210 of 400 passes for 3,145 yards over his college career. He saved some of his best performances for the postseason, lighting up the scoreboard in the Longhorns' 40–27 victory over Missouri (when he accounted for all 40 of his team's points by running, passing and kicking) in the 1946 Cotton Bowl, and the 27–7 victory over sixth-ranked Alabama in the 1948 Sugar Bowl. His stellar 15-year career in the NFL included three league titles. Layne is enshrined in both the College and Pro Football Halls of Fame.

ROOSEVELT LEAKS
Running Back, 1972-74

As a junior in 1973, Leaks finished third in Heisman Trophy voting, the highest finish on record for a UT underclassman. That year he became the first African-American All-American in the school's history after setting the Southwest Conference single-season rushing record with 1,415 yards, averaging 6.2 per carry. A serious knee injury hampered his senior season and professional career—he played nine years for the Baltimore Colts and Buffalo Bills. He still ranks fifth on the Texas career rushing chart, and he is a member of the 2005 class of College Football Hall of Fame inductees.

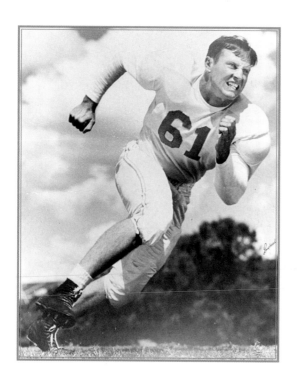

BUD MCFADIN
Guard, 1948-50

Following his senior year in 1950, McFadin was named Southwest Conference Most Valuable Player playing guard on offense and tackle on defense. That fall he led the Longhorns to the conference title and a No. 3 national ranking. He was a two-year All-American and was the MVP of the college All-Star game, which at that time matched the top college players against the reigning NFL champions. McFadin enjoyed an 11-year pro football career and was selected to the Pro Bowl five times.

TOMMY NOBIS
Linebacker-Guard, 1963-65

Tommy Nobis is one of the greatest linebackers who ever lived, and he also played a mean offensive guard as a two-way college standout. He was a three-time All-Southwest Conference honoree and a two-time All-American. He was the only sophomore starter on coach Darrell Royal's 1963 national champion Longhorn team. In the Orange Bowl following his junior season, he registered perhaps the most meaningful tackle in school history, stopping Alabama quarterback Joe Namath at the goal line on fourth-and-inches and saving the 21–17 win for Texas. As a senior, he won both the Outland Trophy and Maxwell Award, averaging almost 20 tackles per game. In the 1966 NFL Draft, he was the number one overall pick by the Atlanta Falcons' expansion franchise, where he earned NFL Rookie of the Year honors in 1966 and was voted to five Pro Bowls. His ongoing absence from the Pro Football Hall of Fame is a glaring omission.

"He'll stay in the buggy when the horse rears up."
DARRELL ROYAL ON TOMMY NOBIS

"I'd rather play against Dick Butkus than Nobis." DOLPHINS RUNNING BACK LARRY CSONKA

JAMES SAXTON
Running Back, 1959-61

Saxton finished third in the Heisman Trophy voting following his brilliant senior season of 1961, when he led the Southwest Conference in rushing with 846 yards on just 107 carries—that's 7.9 yards per carry, the highest in SWC history. He scored on runs of 80, 79, 66, 56, 49 and 45 yards that fall. Darrell Royal called him "the quickest player in America." He concluded his unforgettable senior season by leading the Longhorns to a 12–7 win over fifth-ranked Ole Miss in the 1962 Cotton Bowl. His 73-yard punt on a quick kick that day remains a UT bowl-game record.

HARLEY SEWELL
Guard, 1950-52

Sewell was a two-time All-Southwest Conference selection and an All-America two-way guard as a senior in 1952. He led the 1952 Texas team to a 9–2 record and a 16–0 victory over Tennessee in the Cotton Bowl. Sewell was MVP of the Longhorn defense that held the Vols to six first downs and minus-14 yards rushing. During his pro career in Detroit, he played on two NFL championship teams and was a four-time Pro Bowler.

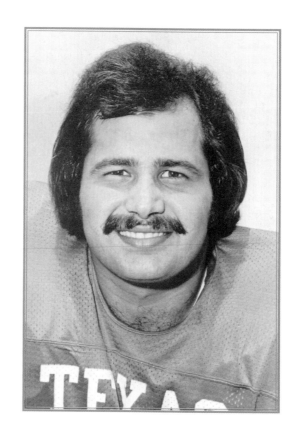

BRAD SHEARER
Defensive Tackle, 1974-77

An Austin native, Shearer was a two-time All-Southwest Conference pick (1975, '77) and a consensus All-American as a senior in 1977. He led the Longhorns that fall with 27 quarterback pressures and four forced fumbles, and registered 109 tackles and seven sacks, during a campaign that found Texas ranked No. 1 in the nation for the entire second half of the regular season. He finished his career with 334 tackles, is third on the school's career charts with 11 forced fumbles and he brought the Outland Trophy home to Austin after his magnificent 1977 season.

Jerry Sisemore
Offensive Tackle, 1970-72

Sisemore was one of the most important contributors during one of the greatest periods of Texas football history. During his three-year playing career in Austin, the Longhorns won three straight Southwest Conference titles and played in three straight Cotton Bowls. He was a sophomore starter for Texas' 1970 national champions and was a two-time consensus All-American as a junior and senior. The Philadelphia Eagles selected him with their first-round pick in the 1973 NFL draft, and he was a two-time Pro Bowl selection, in 1980 and 1982.

MORTIMER "BUD" SPRAGUE
Tackle, 1923-24

In Bud Sprague's junior year of 1923, coach E. J. Stewart's Longhorn team went undefeated with Sprague anchoring the line. Not only was he an All-Southwest Conference tackle in football, but he also excelled in track and field as both a sprinter and a shot putter. He won the conference shot put title in 1925. After graduating from Texas, he continued his football career at Army, where he was a two-time All-American. He was elected to the College Football Hall of Fame in 1970.

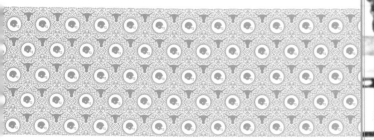

HARRISON STAFFORD
Halfback, 1930-32

Stafford walked on to the Texas freshman football team and freshman coach Shorty Alderson took notice. Alderson reported to head Coach Clyde Littlefield, "Clyde, I found you the darndest football player you ever saw. He tore up a couple of dummies and hurt a couple of men. He says his name is Harrison Stafford." From there, Stafford became a regular on the All-Southwest Conference team for three years. He was the greatest blocking back and probably the toughest football player in Texas history, and he went into the College Football Hall of Fame in 1975.

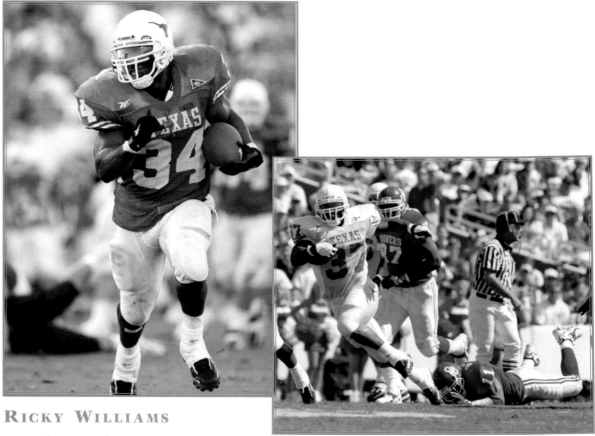

RICKY WILLIAMS
Running Back, 1995-98

In 1995, Williams started at fullback as a true freshman and broke Earl Campbell's school freshman record with 990 yards. As a senior tailback in 1998, Williams seized the NCAA career rushing record in dramatic fashion, with a dazzling 60-yard touchdown run against Texas A&M. He was a two-time All-American and the first player ever to win the Doak Walker Award twice (1997 and '98). His senior year, when he rushed for a school single-season record 2,124 yards, he was named AP Player of the Year and Walter Camp Player of the Year, and won the Maxwell Award and the Heisman Trophy. He averaged 6.2 yards per carry for his career, and his 6,279 rushing yards still rank second in NCAA history.

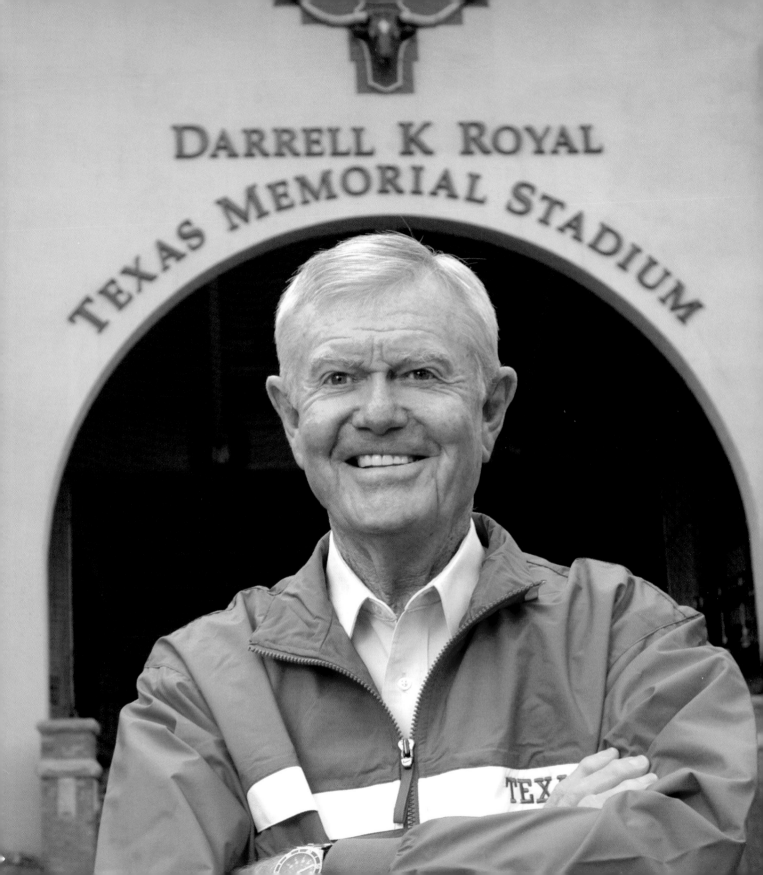

THE GREATEST COACHES

There have been many great coaches over Texas' storied history, including Dana X. Bible, who helped put Longhorn football on the map, and Fred Akers, who coached Earl Campbell to Heisman greatness and guided the Horns to an undefeated regular season in 1977. But two names stand above the rest.

Darrell K. Royal
1957-76

A coach doesn't get a magnificent football stadium named after him unless he's achieved legendary status, and Darrell Royal, whose name was affixed to that of Texas Memorial Stadium in 1996, qualifies as a legend. Royal is the winningest coach in University of Texas history.

After bottoming out at 1–9 in 1956, Texas hired Royal, the former Oklahoma halfback and Mississippi State and Washington head coach, and he produced a 6–4–1 mark right off the bat. In 20 years at Austin, from 1957 to 1976, Royal compiled a record of 167–47–5. During the seasons of 1968 through 1970, his teams won 30 games in a row.

Royal's Longhorns captured 11 Southwest Conference titles and were national champions three times—in 1963, 1969 and 1970. He coached 77 all-conference players and 26 All-Americans.

DARRELL ROYAL YEAR BY YEAR AT TEXAS

YEAR	RECORD	BOWL GAME
1957	6–4–1	Sugar
1958	7–3	
1959*	9–2	Cotton
1960	7–3–1	Bluebonnet
1961*	10–1	Cotton
1962*	9–1–1	Cotton
1963*#	11–0	Cotton
1964	10–1	Orange
1965	6–4	
1966	7–4	Bluebonnet
1967	6–4	
1968*	9–1–1	Cotton
1969*#	11–0	Cotton
1970*#	10–1	Cotton
1971*	8–3	Cotton
1972*	10–1	Cotton
1973*	8–3	Cotton
1974	8–4	Gator
1975*	10–2	Bluebonnet
1976	5–5–1	

* Southwest Conference Champions

National Champions

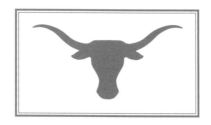

"The finest example of an inspiring world leader I know."* PRESIDENT LYNDON JOHNSON ON TEXAS COACH DARRELL K. ROYAL

Notre Dame coach Ara Parseghian congratulates Darrell K. Royal following Texas' 21-17 win over the Irish in the 1970 Cotton Bowl, which gave the National Champion Longhorns an 11-0 record.

Mack Brown
1998-present

Mack Brown has been a college head coach for 20 years. Before coming to Austin, he had turned North Carolina from double-digit losers (1–10 in both 1988 and '89) into a headliner on the national stage, compiling a record of 20–3 in 1996 and '97. Meanwhile, in Texas, the Longhorns had dipped to 4–7 in 1997, but Brown came to the rescue in 1998. In his first year on the job, he turned in a 9–3 record and a 15th-place ranking in the final AP poll.

Three out of Brown's last four teams have finished in the top 10. Behind Brown's leadership, Texas has captured four postseason victories, including two Cotton Bowl crowns. On New Year's Day, 2005, Brown's Longhorns scored a 38–37 Rose Bowl win over Big Ten champion Michigan. His seven-year record at Texas stands at 70–19, for a winning percentage of .787.

"When you face the Longhorns, I think the first thing that comes to mind is the word 'athleticism.' No matter who leaves in a particular year, Coach (Mack) Brown and his staff do an excellent job of bringing in some of the nation's best athletes. It's a really impressive collection of athletes, and I think much of the country saw that in the Rose Bowl. That may have been a scary preview of things to come." AN OPPOSING BIG 12 COACH ON MACK BROWN AND THE 2005 LONGHORNS

MACK BROWN YEAR-BY-YEAR AT TEXAS

YEAR	RECORD	BOWL GAME
1998	9–3	Cotton
1999	9–5	Cotton
2000	9–3	Holiday
2001	11–2	Holiday
2002	11–2	Cotton
2003	10–3	Holiday
2004	11–1	Rose

"The message we're sending to our team in everything we do—from our off-season workouts to spring practice to the fall—is we want to go back to the Rose Bowl, and we want to win."* MACK BROWN, ON HIS TEAM'S PROSPECTS FOR THE 2005 NATIONAL CHAMPIONSHIP

LONGHORN SUPERLATIVES

Texas football history is littered with moments of greatness—National Championships won, great games played, superior individual efforts, memorable upsets and more. Here is a small sample of that record of achievement.

——— The Championships ———

NATIONAL CHAMPIONSHIPS
1963 (AP, UPI)

Coach Darrell K. Royal's 1963 Texas team opened the campaign with a No. 5 national ranking and quickly shot to the top. After resounding victories in games 1 and 2, the Longhorns found themselves at No. 2 in the nation. They held firm in that spot after a 34–7 win over Oklahoma State, setting up the annual battle with Oklahoma in Dallas. The Sooners were the nation's top-ranked team going in, but the Horns took the top spot from them with a 28–7 victory.

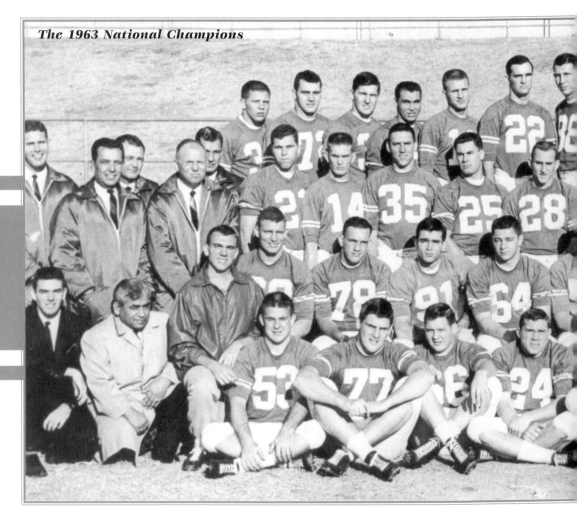

The 1963 National Champions

The biggest play of the season might have come four weeks later in the Baylor game. Duke Carlisle saved Texas' season that day with a sensational leaping interception of a potential game-tying touchdown pass from Baylor's Don Trull to Lawrence Elkins with 29 seconds left. The Texas A&M contest was another white-knuckler—a 15–13 victory after trailing the Aggies 13–3 to start the fourth quarter. Carlisle scored the winning touchdown with 1:19 to play. The finishing touch on the title was a 28–6 Cotton Bowl victory

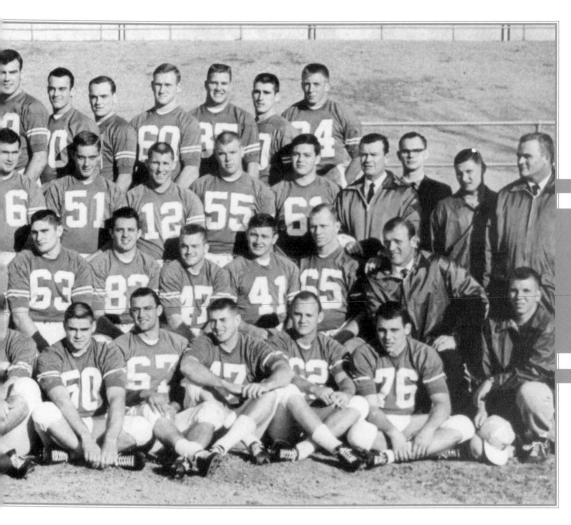

over second-ranked Navy, quarterbacked by that year's Heisman winner, Roger Staubach. Carlisle connected with Phil Harris on touchdown passes of 58 and 63 yards in the win. Tommy Ford led the Longhorns' 1963 rushing attack with 763 yards; tackle Scott Appleton was a consensus All-American and won the Outland Trophy. Linebacker Tommy Nobis enjoyed a sensational sophomore campaign, two years before winning the 1965 Maxwell Award as the nation's outstanding player.

The 1969 National Champions

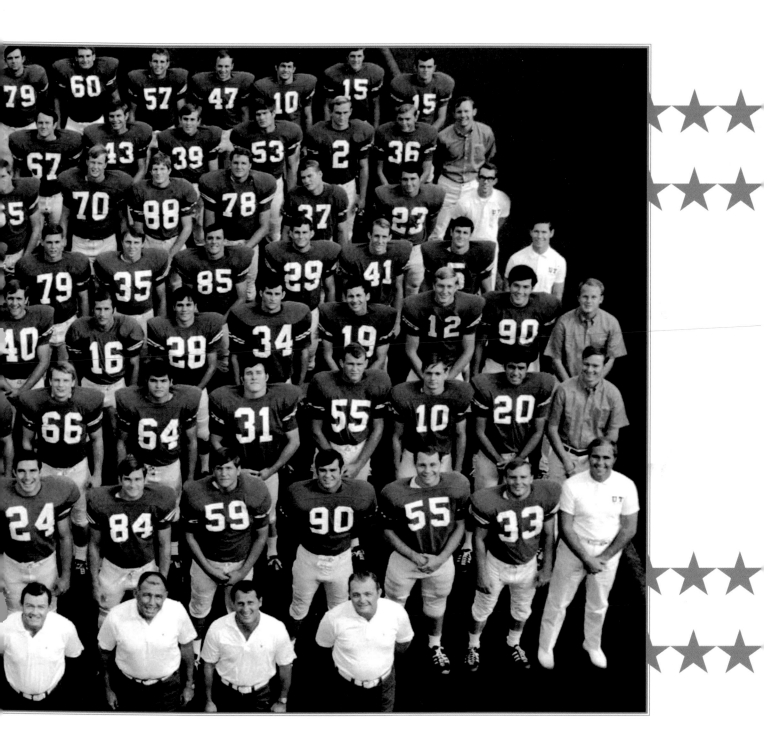

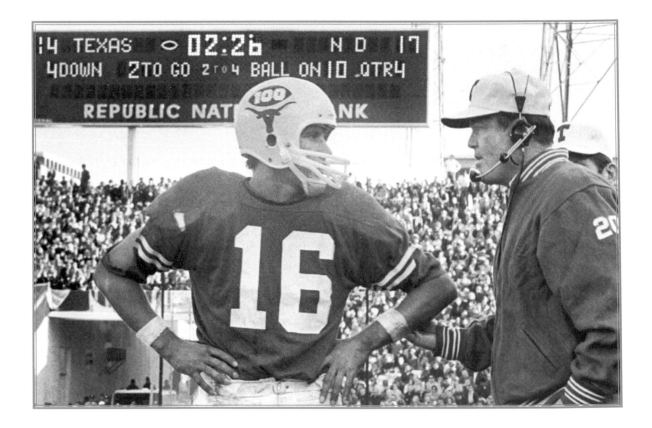

1969 (AP, UPI)

Just as in 1963, Texas' 1969 national title campaign involved a No. 1 vs. No. 2 matchup. This time Arkansas was the opponent in a game that ABC-TV had moved from Oct. 18 to Dec. 6. It took an assist from Michigan, which defeated top-ranked Ohio State on Nov. 22, to vault the Longhorns over the Buckeyes to the top spot in the polls. A 15–14 Texas win over the second-ranked Razorbacks in the regular-season finale followed by a 21–17 Cotton Bowl victory over Notre Dame left little doubt among fans and pollsters as to who the champion of college football was that year. A spotless 11–0 record didn't hurt, either.

Any list of "Games of the Century" that does not include the 1969 Texas-Arkansas game is of no interest. UT quarterback James

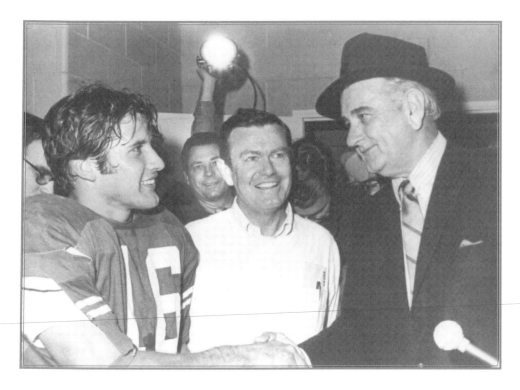

Street ran for a touchdown and a two-point conversion that day, and connected with receiver Randy Peschel on a crucial fourth-and-3 play late in the game. In the victors' locker room following the game, President Richard Nixon awarded the Texas team a plaque emblematic of the National Championship.

On New Year's Day, Texas trailed coach Ara Parseghian's Fighting Irish 17–14 midway through the fourth quarter when Street piloted the Longhorns 76 yards to the winning score, with Billy Dale doing the honors from 1 yard out.

All season long, Street masterfully guided the wishbone offense, then in its second year of existence. The 1969 Longhorns led the nation in rushing with 363 yards per contest. In the SMU game, the Horns rushed for 611 yards, with Street, halfbacks Jim Bertelsen and Ted Koy, and fullback Steve Worster each surpassing the century mark. Worster, wide receiver Cotton Speyrer, linebacker Glen Halsell and tackles Bob McKay and Bobby Wuensch were All-Americans.

1970 (UPI)

Texas entered the 1970 season defending a national championship and sitting on a 20-game winning streak, yet were ranked second nationally and remained there until claiming the top spot in late October. It took a game-winning, 45-yard touchdown pass from quarterback Eddie Phillips to Cotton Speyrer with 12 seconds remaining against 13th-ranked UCLA to pull out a 20–17 win and extend the Longhorns' winning streak to 23.

The following week, Texas pounded Oklahoma 49–9. That win and the 45–21 victory over Rice the following week promoted the Horns to No. 1, a position they never relinquished. The regular season concluded with blowout victories over Texas A&M (52–14) and fourth-ranked Arkansas (42–7).

The 1970 Texas team had ridden its wishbone offense to a 10–0 mark, a third consecutive Southwest Conference championship and a date with sixth-ranked Notre Dame in the Cotton Bowl. The Irish stopped Texas winning streak at 30 games on New Year's Day, 1971, and dropped the Longhorns to No. 3 in the AP poll. But the UPI poll was closed after the regular season, locking Texas in as national champion.

The 1970 Longhorns outdid themselves, topping the previous season's incredible rushing output with a still-standing school record 374.5 yards per game on the ground. Fullback Steve Worster, wide receiver Cotton Speyrer, offensive tackle Bobby Wuensch, defensive end Bill Atessis and linebacker Scott Henderson were All-Americans. The "Worster crowd," the fabulous freshmen class of 1967, concluded their college careers with a record of 30-2-1.

Texas' loss to Notre Dame in the Cotton Bowl scarcely diminished the accomplishments of the "Worster Crowd": Steve Worster, Cotton Speyrer, Bobby Wuensch, Bill Atessis, Scott Henderson, et al.—a group that posted a three-year record of 30-2-1.

The 1970 National Champions

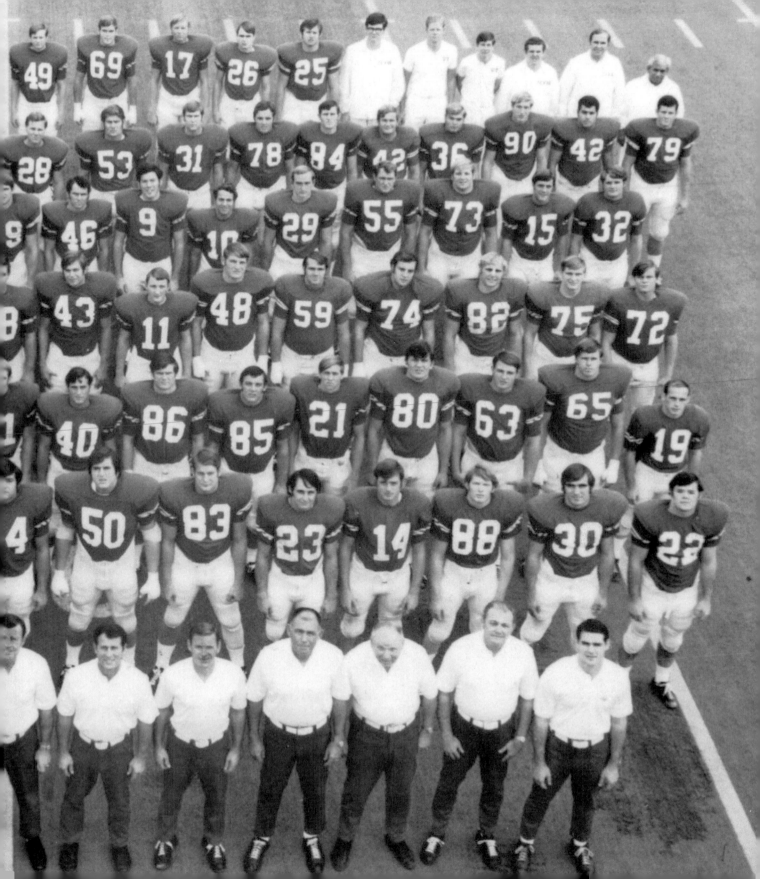

CONFERENCE CHAMPIONSHIPS (26)

YEAR	CONFERENCE	OVERALL
1920	5–0–0 (SWC)	9–0–0
1928	5–1–0 (SWC)	7–2–0
1930	4–1–0 (SWC)	8–1–1
1942	5–1–0 (SWC)	9–2–0
1943	5–0–0 (SWC)	7–1–1
1945	5–1–0 (SWC)	10–1–0
1950	6–0–0 (SWC)	9–2–0
1952	6–0–0 (SWC)	9–2–0
*1953	5–1–0 (SWC)	7–3–0
*1959	5–1–0 (SWC)	9–2–0
*1961	6–1–0 (SWC)	10–1–0
1962	6–0–1 (SWC)	9–1–1
1963	7–0–0 (SWC)	11–0–0
*1968	6–1–0 (SWC)	9–1–1
1969	7–0–0 (SWC)	11–0–0
1970	7–0–0 (SWC)	10–1–0
1971	6–1–0 (SWC)	8–3–0
1972	7–0–0 (SWC)	10–1–0
1973	7–0–0 (SWC)	8–3–0
*1975	6–1–0 (SWC)	10–2–0
1977	8–0–0 (SWC)	11–1–0
1983	8–0–0 (SWC)	11–1–0
1990	8–0–0 (SWC)	10–2–0
*1994	4–3–0 (SWC)	8–4–0
1995	7–0–0 (SWC)	10–2–1
1996	6–2–0 (Big 12)	8–5–0

*co-championships

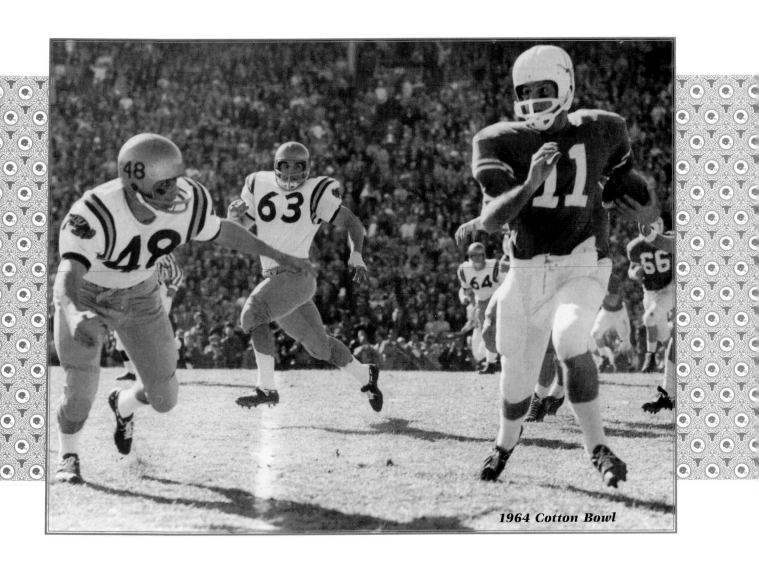

1964 Cotton Bowl

Greatest Games

TEXAS 7, TEXAS A&M 3
NOV. 25, 1920

The largest crowd ever to see a football game in the state of Texas to that point, some 20,000 strong, crammed the stands at Clark Field to witness this historic matchup. Texas was undefeated and unchallenged, having outscored its previous eight opponents that year 275–10. The Aggies hadn't been scored on in two years. The buzz surrounding the game could be heard nationwide. A&M kicked a field goal in the second quarter to go up 3–0. With time running out in the game, Texas ran a halfback reverse, tackle eligible play, with Bill Barry throwing and tackle Tom Dennis making a one-handed circus catch, putting the Longhorns in business at the four. Francis Domingues ran the ball into the end zone on the next play. The 7–3 victory closed an undefeated season for the Longhorns and put an end to A&M's two-year unbeaten streak.

TEXAS 15, OKLAHOMA 14
OCT. 11, 1958

Texas came into the 1958 Oklahoma game as a heavy underdog and mired in a six-game losing streak in the series. But the Longhorns drew first blood on a 10-yard touchdown pass from Bobby Lackey to Rene Ramirez and pulled the rug out from under the Sooners with a two-point conversion to go up 8–0. A third quarter OU touchdown brought the score to 8–6, and a 24-yard fumble recovery by Jim Davis put Oklahoma up 14–8 early in the fourth quarter. Texas took possession with 6:50 left in the game, and backup quarterback Vince Matthews drove the Longhorns from their own 26 to the OU 7. Lackey came back in the game, found receiver Bobby Bryant with a jump pass to tie the game with 3:10 remaining, kicked the extra point and intercepted an Oklahoma pass to put the game away.

A milestone of the Royal era: Texas' 15-14 win over Oklahoma in 1958

TEXAS 7, ARKANSAS 3
OCT. 20, 1962

The top-ranked Longhorns welcomed seventh-ranked Arkansas to Memorial Stadium for a crucial Southwest Conference matchup in 1962. Both teams were sporting 4–0 records. The Razorbacks took an early 3–0 lead and held it into the third quarter. Coach Frank Broyles' team drove methodically downfield to the Texas 5-yard line. On second down fullback Danny Brabham plunged into the line from the three, where Texas' Johnny Treadwell and Pat Culpepper met him head-on (left). The ball popped loose and Texas recovered in the end zone for a touchback. The Hogs got the ball back but the Longhorns stopped them on fourth and one at the Texas 12. From there, quarterback Duke Carlisle led the Horns downfield on an 88-yard drive, culminating in Tommy Ford's 3-yard game-winning touchdown run with 36 seconds left in the game.

TEXAS 21, ALABAMA 17
JAN. 1, 1965

Ernie Koy led Texas with 133 yards rushing in the 1965 Orange Bowl as the fifth-ranked Longhorns defeated top-ranked Alabama 21–17, ruining an otherwise perfect season for Bear Bryant's team. Texas took a 21–7 lead into halftime and hung on for the win. 'Bama quarterback Joe Namath completed 18 of 37 passes for 255 yards and two touchdowns, but the Texas ground game, led by Koy, sliced through the Crimson Tide defense for 212 yards while the UT defense held Alabama to just 49 yards on the ground.

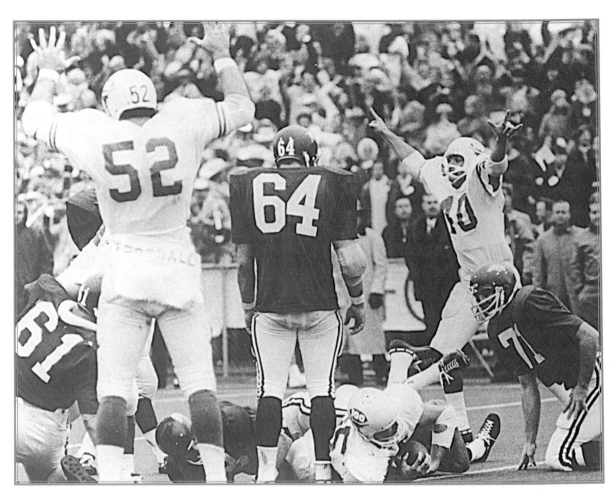

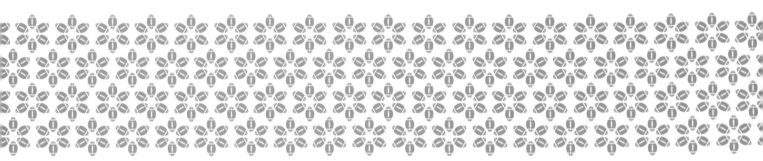

TEXAS 15, ARKANSAS 14
DEC. 6, 1969

Top-ranked Texas took an 18-game winning streak into its 1969 matchup with second-ranked Arkansas, which was riding a 15-game winning streak of its own. President Richard Nixon was present to crown the winner national champion by proclamation. Texas led the nation in rushing; Arkansas boasted the nation's stingiest defense. The Razorbacks led 7–0 at the half and stretched the lead to 14–0 on a 29-yard Bill Montgomery-to-Chuck Dicus touchdown pass in the third quarter. Later in the third, Texas quarterback James Street galloped 42 yards for a touchdown, tacking on a two-point conversion to cut the margin to 14–8. Moments later Arkansas drove to the Texas 7, where Danny Lester intercepted a Montgomery pass in the end zone. Texas fumbled the ball away but got it back on its own 38 with 7:58 remaining in the game. On fourth and three from the Longhorn 43, Street hit Randy Peschel with a 44-yard strike. Two plays later, Jim Bertelsen scored from the 2. Happy Feller's PAT put the Horns up 15–14, and Tom Campbell's interception of a desperation pass by Montgomery with 1:22 showing on the clock sealed the win.

TEXAS 17, ALABAMA 13
JAN. 1, 1973

Darrell K. Royal's Longhorns defeated Bear Bryant's Crimson Tide 17–13 in a battle of top-10 teams in the 1973 Cotton Bowl. Alabama led 13–3 at halftime, but the second half belonged to the hosts from the Southwest Conference. Quarterback Alan Lowry, run-ning back Roosevelt Leaks and offensive tackle Jerry Sisemore led the second-half comeback. For the game, Leaks ran for 120 yards with Lowry adding 117 on the ground and 61 through the air. Lowry's 34-yard touchdown run on a bootleg with 4:22 left in the game provided the winning points.

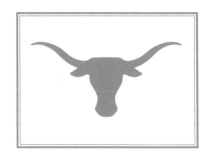

TEXAS 14, ALABAMA 12
JAN. 1, 1982

In the 1982 Cotton Bowl game, sixth-ranked Texas took on third-ranked Alabama with both teams sporting 9–1–1 records. 'Bama held a 10–0 lead in the fourth quarter when Texas quarterback Robert Brewer shocked the football watching nation with a 70-yard touchdown run—with a quarterback draw on third and long. The Longhorns' next possession, an 11-play, 80-yard march, culminated in Terry Orr's 8-yard touchdown run for a 14–10 Texas lead with 2:05 left in the game. Following a Texas interception at its own 1, the Horns decided to play the field position game and took a safety with time running out to make the final score 14–12.

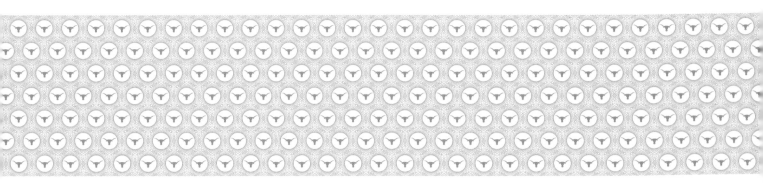

TEXAS 15, SMU 12
OCT. 22, 1983

Both Texas and SMU entered their 1983 contest at 5–0, with the Mustangs unbeaten in their last 21 outings. The Longhorns were ranked second nationally. Texas survived a turnover-plagued performance and had to rally from behind twice. With the score tied 6–6 on two field goals apiece, quarterback Todd Dodge led the Longhorns downfield to the SMU 7, then hit Bill Boy Bryant with a scoring strike to go up 13–6 early in the fourth quarter. SMU responded with a touchdown to cap an 80-yard drive, but Jerry Gray batted down Lance McIlhenny's two-point conversion pass attempt. Texas tacked on a safety with the game clock winding down and escaped Texas Stadium in Dallas with a 15–12 win.

TEXAS 37, NEBRASKA 27
DEC. 7, 1996

It was the inaugural Big 12 Championship game, and unranked Texas entered as a three-touchdown underdog to third-ranked Nebraska. The Cornhuskers were two-time defending national champions, but UT quarterback James Brown's 353 yards on 19 of 28 passing put an end to that. Priest Holmes led the Longhorn ground attack. One of the most memorable plays in Texas history—a 61-yard rollout pass from Brown to tight end Derek Lewis on fourth-and-inches—came with 2:48 left in the game. Holmes scored on an 11-yard run on the following play to put the game away.

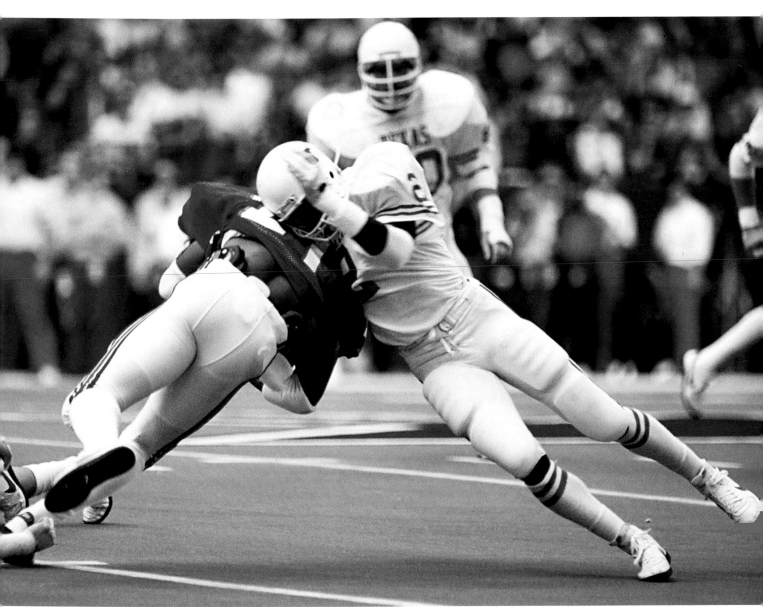

TEXAS 26, TEXAS A&M 24
NOV. 27, 1998

The 105th meeting between Texas and Texas A&M drew a record crowd of 83,687 and a national television audience. Not only would Ricky Williams' quest for the all-time NCAA rushing title come to fruition that day, but the game itself was a memorable one. The Longhorns took a 23–7 lead, but the Aggies stormed back to go ahead 24–23 with just 2:20 left in the game. Major Applewhite's passing brought the Horns to within field-goal range as the clock was winding down. Kris Stockton kicked the game-winning 24-yarder for the 26–24 upset win. Along the way, Williams broke Tony Dorsett's 22-year old NCAA career rushing record on a scintillating 60-yard touchdown run. Williams ran for 259 yards that day against an Aggie defense that was allowing just 104.8 per game on the ground.

TEXAS 47, WASHINGTON 43
DEC. 28, 2001

Texas quarterback Major Applewhite set Texas bowl game passing records with 37 completions on 55 attempts for 473 yards and four touchdowns in the 2001 Holiday Bowl shootout. Roy Williams' 11 catches set another school postseason mark. Washington jumped out to a 13–0 lead, then Texas came back to go ahead 14–13 in the second quarter. Midway through the third period, the Longhorns were trailing by 19 points when they mounted a 30–7 run and scored on four of their final five possessions for the 47–43 win. Freshman linebacker Derrick Johnson racked up nine tackles, a sack and a key fourth-quarter interception.

TEXAS 27, NEBRASKA 24
NOV. 2, 2003

Chris Simms passed for 419 yards and Roy Williams caught 13 passes for 161 yards and two touchdowns as the Longhorns halted the Cornhuskers' 26-game home winning streak, the nation's longest at the time. With Texas protecting a 27–24 lead, a 10-yard pass from Simms to Williams for a first down with 1:34 remaining in the game was negated by a penalty. DeJuan Groce returned the ensuing punt for the Huskers 44 yards to Texas' 16. Two snaps later, Texas cornerback Nathan Vasher saved the day, leaping high in the air to intercept Husker quarterback Jammal Lord at the 1-yard line and seal the win.

Greatest Moments

ECKHARDT'S RUN
OCT. 20, 1923

Back in the day when Vanderbilt claimed one of the nation's top football programs, the Commodores rolled into Dallas for a game with Texas at the State Fair. Late in the game, Texas had the ball on the Vandy 20. Longhorn back Oscar Eckhardt took the snap and headed for the sideline, then downfield, plowing through practically the entire Vanderbilt team to the 8, where he almost went down. When he regained his balance, he continued to flatten Commodore defenders, keeping never more than a yard inside the sideline, until he finally hit paydirt and salted away the 16–0 win.

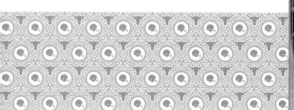

THE IMPOSSIBLE CATCH
NOV. 28, 1940

Texas A&M rolled into Memorial Stadium with a 19-game winning streak for its annual Thanksgiving Day game with the Longhorns. On the third play of the game, Texas' Noble Doss made what is known to Longhorn fans as "the impossible catch," to set up the only score of the day—a one-yard run by Pete Layden on the next play. The 7–0 Texas win knocked the Aggies out of the Rose Bowl and spoiled their dreams of repeating as national champions.

CARLISLE TO THE RESCUE
NOV. 9, 1963

Texas was 7–0 and appeared to be sailing to the national title when it ran into 5–1 Baylor, quarterbacked by Don Trull. Texas led 7–0 with 29 seconds left in the game when Trull saw his favorite receiver, Lawrence Elkins, wide open near the goal line on a post pattern for an apparent 19-yard touchdown pass. Longhorn quarterback-safety Duke Carlisle closed in on Elkins from 15 yards away after Trull released the ball to make the season-saving interception.

86 PASS, TED CROSSING, SAM POST
OCT. 3, 1970

Texas' 22-game winning streak was in jeopardy at home in Austin against UCLA. The Longhorns trailed 17–13 with 25 seconds remaining in the game and 45 yards separating them from victory. Quarterback Eddie Phillips called "86 pass, Ted crossing, Sam post" in the huddle and hit Cotton Speyrer over the middle at the 20. Speyrer spun free of the Bruin defender and raced to paydirt with 12 seconds left in the game. The Longhorns stretched their winning streak to 23 and repeated as national champions.

"LOOK TO RUN"
DEC. 7, 1996

The Longhorns were on their way to a monumental upset, leading two-time defending national champion Nebraska 30–27 but needing to eat up the last 2:40 of game clock. On fourth-and-inches with the ball at their own 28, Texas called timeout. Coach John Mackovic and quarterback James Brown decided on a play called "Steeler Roll Left," in which the quarterback can pass or take off running at his own discretion. Mackovic concluded the sideline conference with the words, "Look to run." But as the play developed, Brown found tight end Derek Lewis wide open for a 61-yard completion. On the next play, Priest Holmes scored from 11 yards out and the Longhorns came away with 37–27 win in the inaugural Big 12 Championship game.

Texas QB James Brown leads a monumental upset of Nebraska

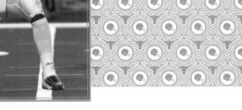

RICKY'S RUN TO THE RECORD
NOV. 27, 1998

The historic Texas-Texas A&M rivalry took on even greater significance than usual. Ricky Williams entered the 1998 matchup with the Aggies needing 62 yards to break Tony Dorsett's 22-year-old NCAA career rushing record of 6,082 yards. Dorsett himself along with Roger Clemens were among the sports dignitaries who populated the Texas sideline that afternoon to witness the event. With 1:13 left in the first quarter, only 11 yards remained to go. First and 10. The play was "L King Zin 53." Williams took the handoff from Major Applewhite, broke three tackles and sprinted his way 60 yards to history. The Longhorns won the game 26–24.

1977 Texas Longhorns

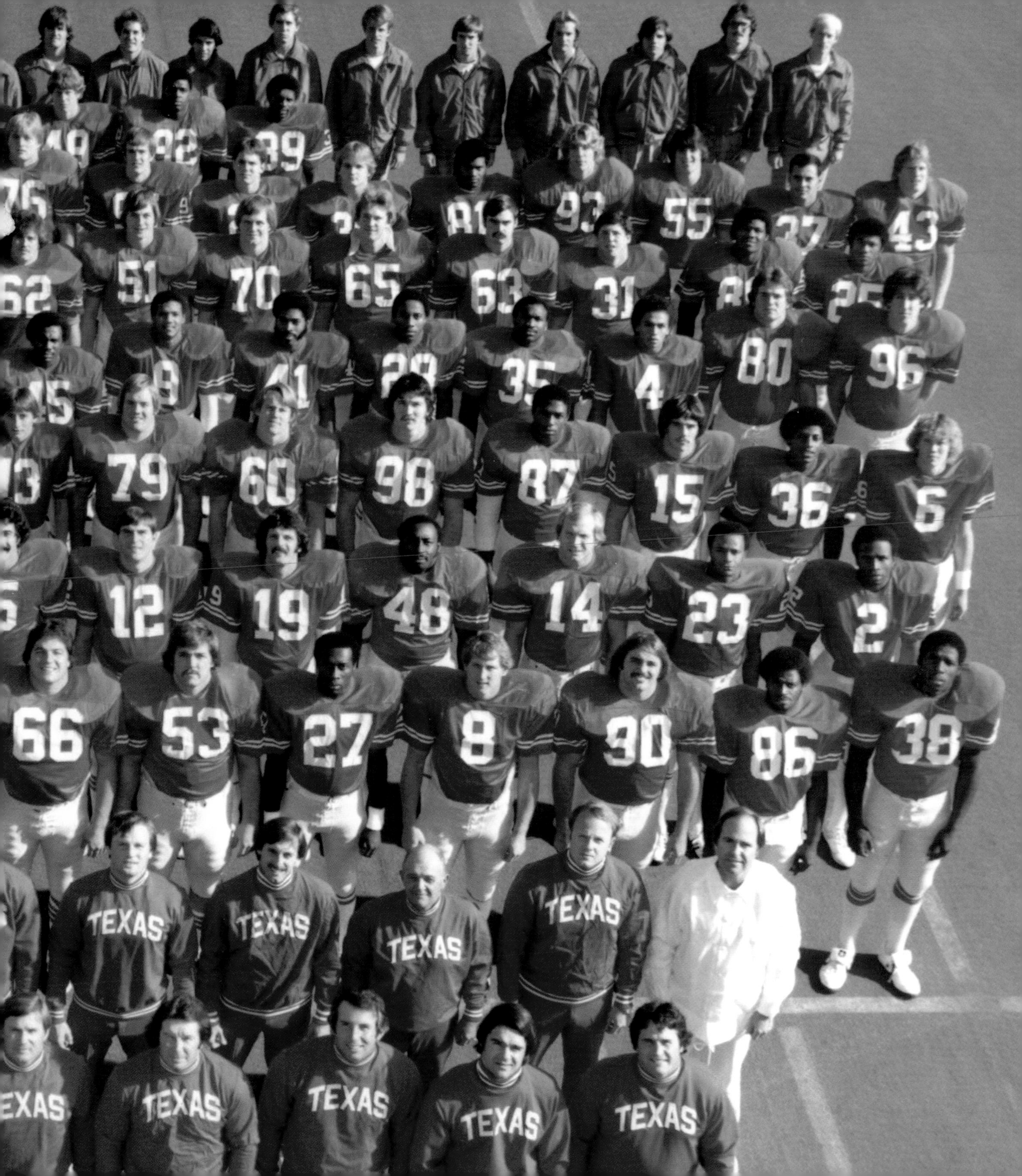
TEXAS
TEXAS
TEXAS
TEXAS
TEXAS
TEXAS
TEXAS
TEXAS
TEXAS

THE RIVALRIES

Two great rivalries have helped define Texas football and have given fans many of their greatest memories.

The Red River Shootout

Oil wells have been known to change hands as a result of wagers on the outcome. The game is played every year at a neutral site—Dallas, Texas. Oil country. And the graduates and devotees of both schools, Texas and Oklahoma, raise the stakes off the field almost as high as those riding on the game itself.

The backdrop is the Texas State Fair. Cotton Bowl Stadium. Second weekend of October. Fan entourages equally divided between those arrayed in crimson and those in burnt orange, the line of demarcation drawn sharply down the 50-yard line. The Red River Shootout.

A major bowl atmosphere surrounds this event when two of the most tradition-gorged programs in college football battle it out. Between the two, they have won 10 national championships.

But it wasn't always so. The two schools first met on the gridiron in 1900, seven years before Oklahoma was admitted to the union as a state. Texas won that first contest 28–2, and the next four after that, including two in 1901. Texas, then known as the Steers, treated the Oklahoma game as a practice workout. But it was just a matter of time before Oklahoma became competitive on a national level.

Until the inception of the Big 12 in 1996, Texas-Oklahoma had been an interconference game since OU jumped from the Southwest Conference to the Big Six (later to become the Big Eight) in 1920. The game moved permanently to the Texas State Fair in 1929 and from the outset was the main event. Texas won that first meeting in Dallas 21–0, with the Longhorns in the midst of a six-game winning streak over the Sooners.

In 1947, Texas owned a 27–9–2 lead in the series. Then Oklahoma coach Jim Tatum left for Maryland and assistant Bud Wikinson was elevated to head coach. The Sooners dominated the Horns during the first decade of Wilkinson's reign, winning eight of the first 10 matchups. OU's NCAA-record 47-game winning streak from 1953 to 1957 included five wins over Texas.

In 1950, the national title was on the line. Texas led 13–7 in the fourth quarter, but a fumbled punt snap gave the Sooners the ball in the shadow of the Texas goal post. Billy Vessels, who would win the Heisman Trophy for the Sooners two years later, slashed off tackle for the winning touchdown in the 14–7 win, and the Sooners were national champs.

After finishing 1–9 in 1956, Texas brought in Darrell K. Royal as coach, and the Longhorns' football fortunes took a dramatic upswing. Royal's first Texas team lost to the Sooners 21–7, but the Longhorns won the next six until Wilkinson's retirement in 1963. Final tally: Royal 6, Wilkinson 1.

In 1958, Texas had lost six in a row to Wilkinson's Sooners and entered the contest 13-point underdogs. The Longhorns took an 8–0 lead on a 10-yard touchdown pass from Bobby Lackey to Rene Ramirez and a two-point conversion. The NCAA had changed the rules that year to allow teams to go for 2, hoping to reduce the number of ties, and Royal had opposed the change. But without it, his club could not have pulled off the 15–14 upset win.

In 1963, Wilkinson's final season at the helm in Norman, No. 1 Oklahoma and No. 2 Texas squared off in what was anticipated as the Game of the Century. Scott Appleton, the All-America Texas tackle who finished fifth in the Heisman voting that year, racked up 18 tackles in the game as the Horns rolled to a 28–7 victory and the No. 1 ranking. Texas finished the '63 season 11–0 and national champions.

In 1968, Texas unleashed the wishbone, at the time called the Y formation, on the football world. It was the brainchild of Royal's backfield coach, Emory Bellard, who had been under instructions to devise a scheme to get Texas' two great fullbacks—Ted Koy and Steve Worster—into the backfield at the same time with halfback Chris Gilbert, the first player in NCAA history to rush for 1,000 yards in each year of his eligibility.

The first time the Sooners saw the odd formation, in the 1968 Red River Shootout, they were holding on to a 20–19 lead with 2:37 remaining and had Texas backed up on its own 15. But Longhorn quarterback James Street rose to the challenge, with four pass completions to lead his team to the Sooners' 21 with 55 seconds to play. From there, Worster took over, rumbling 14 yards on one run, then 7 yards for the winning touchdown and the 26–20 win.

1963's Game of the Century: No. 2 Texas dismantles No. 1 Oklahoma en route to the National Championship.

to score.

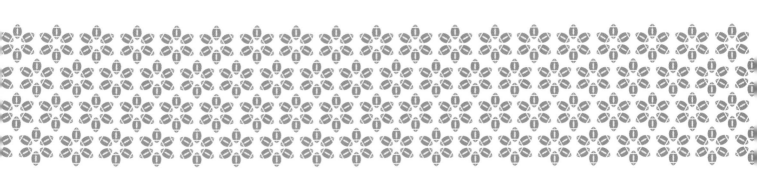

In 1976, Royal was in his final year at Texas. Oklahoma was two-time defending national champion under Barry Switzer, now in his fourth season. That '76 contest, which ended in a 6–6 tie, was surrounded by allegations of skullduggery on the part of Switzer, who was accused of sending a spy to Texas' practices. Accusations and denials flew hot and heavy. Royal and the Longhorn faithful already resented the fact that Oklahoma's rosters were regularly stocked with former Texas schoolboy stars, many of whom had been instrumental in defeating their home-state team over the years. Royal, by the way, is an Oklahoma native and was an All-America quarterback in the late-'40s at OU, where Wilkinson was his coach.

Red River Classic

Score: Texas 13, Oklahoma 6

Date: October 8, 1977

Details: Fifth-ranked Texas had endured six years of frustration against Oklahoma, which entered Texas State Fair week ranked No. 2. Texas ended the frustration in storybook fashion.

UT starting quarterback Mark McBath and backup John Aune both went down in the first quarter with season-ending injuries, setting the stage for little-used junior Randy McEachern, who went into the season not even listed in the Texas media guide. McEachern led the Horns on an 80-yard touchdown drive just before halftime to give Texas a 10–3 lead.

Russell Erxleben put Texas up 13–6 with a 58-yard field goal (after converting a 64-yarder in the first half!) with 8:08 left. Oklahoma then drove to the Texas 4-yard line, where it faced a fourth-and-one with 4:10 to go. Sooner QB Thomas Lott was nailed by UT All-Americans Brad Shearer and Johnny Johnson for no gain. OU forced a Texas punt, but Erxleben launched a 69-yarder from his own end zone to end the danger. Earl Campbell was one of many Longhorn heroes, rushing for 124 yards, including a 24-yard run for Texas' only TD.

Texas won the 1983 matchup 28–16, and an all-time record 17 Longhorns were drafted into the NFL following that season. Despite the graduation losses, Texas entered the 1984 renewal with a No. 1 ranking. On a rain-soaked Cotton Bowl field, the Longhorns took a 10–0 halftime lead on a Todd Dodge touchdown pass and a 40-yard Jeff Ward field goal. In the third quarter, the Sooners capitalized on a Texas fumble to pull within three points, 10–7. Moments later, a safety brought the score to 10–9, then Oklahoma took a 15–10 lead on a 24-yard Danny Bradley touchdown pass. A two-point conversion attempt failed. Midway through the fourth quarter, freshman tailback Kevin Nelson splashed 60 yards through the mud to put the Horns in business on the Oklahoma 2, where the Sooner defense mounted a goal-line stand. OU took over at the 3 but couldn't move the ball either. Then Switzer, not trusting his punting game, decided to call an inten-

tional safety, and the score went to 15–12 Oklahoma. After the free kick, Dodge passed the Horns to the Sooner 15 with 10 seconds left. A field goal tied the game at 15, and that's how it ended. Mack Brown, Texas' current head coach, was offensive coordinator for Oklahoma in that 1984 game.

Texas entered the 1989 contest having not beaten the Sooners in six years. The Longhorns' 21–7 halftime advantage turned into a 24–21 Oklahoma lead in the fourth quarter. But with less than two minutes to play, Texas quarterback Peter Gardere fired a 25-yard strike to an outstretched Johnny Walker for the winning touchdown and the Longhorns escaped with a 28–24 victory. The following year, Texas put together another late-fourth-quarter game-wining touchdown drive, this time a 91-yard gem. Again the winning points came off Gardere's arm, a 16-yard dart to Keith Cash for the 14–13 victory.

In 1993, Oklahoma coach Gary Gibbs entered the game with an 0–4 record against Texas and a gimpy quarterback in Cale Gundy, who had suffered a hip injury that week in practice. But Gundy came through like a trooper, rushing for three touchdowns in the Sooners' 38–17 win. By 1996, John Blake had taken over as coach at OU, and the Sooners were 0–4 on the season. But Oklahoma prevailed over John Mackovic's Texans in overtime 30–27, and Blake had his first victory as the Sooners' head man.

Mackovic's last Texas team, in 1997, and Mack Brown's first, in 1998, both defeated the Sooners. Brown's Red River victory in his inaugural season at the helm was a 34–3 thumping. He followed it up with a 38–28 win over the Sooners in 1999, Bob Stoops' first season as the head man in Norman. Entering the 2005 matchup, Oklahoma is riding a five-game winning streak in the series. But present-day Longhorn legends Vince Young and Rod Wright can swing the pendulum back the other way and add their own names to the lore of this great historic rivalry.

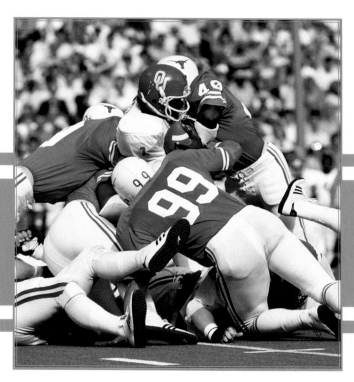

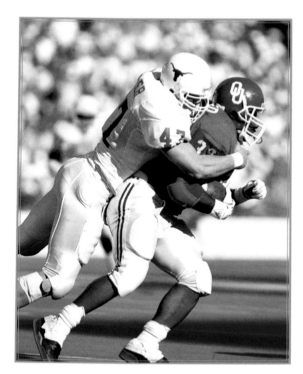

"Good players play their best in Texas-OU games. The adrenaline's really flowing. If you got any fight in you, your neck gets a little redder that day, regardless of which side you're on." DARRELL K. ROYAL, ON THE RED RIVER RIVALRY

Texas A&M

When it comes to in-state rivalries, Alabama-Auburn has nothing on this one. To say folks in the Lone Star State take the Texas-Texas A&M rivalry seriously is an understatement. They take it personally.

The University of Texas began playing football in 1893 and began whipping up on Texas A&M in the season opener the following year. The Varsity, as the Texas teams of the early days were called, beat the Aggies 38–0. The Varsity won the first seven games in the series, all shutouts, and 14 of the first 17.

And then Charley Moran arrived in College Station. We can picture him riding onto the Aggie campus astride a white horse, six-shooters strapped to his waist, "Beat Texas" buttons pinned to his tunic. This was 1909 and Moran was the Aggies' 10th football coach. Moran's first words were, "I didn't come here to lose."

He didn't. Moran is the only Aggie coach whose teams defeated Texas twice in one year. By the middle of 1910, his second season, the Aggies had a 10-game winning streak. Moran had lit the fire.

Texas authorities suspected a rat in the woodpile and, sure enough, one of Moran's stars admitted later that "from time to time we used boys of questionable academic pedigree."

Texas broke off relations, diplomatic and otherwise, with the Aggies after the 1911 game. A verse chanted in the saloons of Austin shows what Texas students and fans thought of Moran:

To hell, to hell with Charley Moran
And all his dirty crew
And if you don't like the words of this song
To hell, to hell with you

When the school decided to resume combat in 1915, Moran was fired, probably in a concession to the powerful politicos at Texas—but the Longhorns had not heard the last of Charley Moran.

From exile in Kentucky, Moran wrote each Aggie player, urging him to "beat those people from Austin, if you still love me and think anything of me."

There must have been something of a mystic hangover from the Moran years, because in the first game after his departure, the Longhorns fumbled 12 times and A&M won 13–0. The next year, Texas avenged that loss 21–7 and celebrated by acquiring a mascot, a Longhorn steer.

In 1909, Moran's first year at the helm of the program, a tradition was born that would grow into *Guinness Book* proportions. From its modest beginnings, the Texas A&M bonfire the night before the Texas game grew into monsters of well over 100 feet tall. But since the tragedy of Nov. 18, 1999, when the center pole snapped during construction and the entire structure collapsed, killing 12 students, the bonfire was discontinued and has yet to reappear on the landscape.

By 1920, the game had become an annual crusade for players, students and fans of both schools. A paragraph in the 1920 Texas student newspaper says it all: "The A&M game is at hand and classes and quizzes are mere details."

A&M hired Dana X. Bible, who later would "jump ship" and, after eight years at Nebraska, become a legend at Texas, where he coached 10 years.

The Aggies knew Bible had built something in 1920 when his team wiped out Daniel Baker 110–0 in the season opener. By the time the Aggies arrived in Austin for the last game of the year, they hadn't yielded a single point.

That 1920 contest was surely one of the greatest in the history of the series. Maybe it was even, as the *Austin American Statesman* declared, "the greatest athletic contest ever played in Texas." You can imagine players bashing noses, denting leather helmets, wiping the blood off their knuckles on moleskin pants.

What the Aggies couldn't imagine was Texas scoring a touchdown in the fourth quarter for a 7–3 victory, winding up a perfect 9–0 season. In a sneak preview of things to come much later, the Longhorns, exasperated after hammering at the Aggie defense all afternoon, pulled a trick pass play. They made tackle Tom Dennis eligible with a quick shift, and he caught a pass at the A&M 3. Texas scored on the next play, bringing the first of 25 Southwest Conference titles to Austin.

Two years later, Bible used a shift of his own—to the history books. At halftime in Austin, where the Aggies had never won, Bible reminded his squad of the Alamo legend where Colonel William B. Travis supposedly drew a line in the dirt floor and invited all who wanted to stay and fight the huge Mexican force to step across the line and join him.

"Now men," Bible said, screeching a chalk line across the locker room floor, "those who want to become known as the first A&M team to defeat Texas in Austin, step over the line."

Bible was almost trampled in the rush, and the Aggies broke the 7–7 halftime tie and won 14–7.

From 1925 to 1939, neither team could put together two wins in a row over the other. Then the Longhorns won eight in a row from 1940 to 1947. And then, after Bear Bryant left Texas A&M and Darrell Royal arrived at Texas with the makings of a dynasty, the Longhorns began to take charge of the series. They reeled off 10 straight wins, until in 1967 Edd Hargett threw an 80-yard missile to Bob Long that propelled the Aggies to a 10–7 victory and the conference title.

Coach Bible

"There were several years when we didn't have the manpower to keep up with Texas," remembered Gene Stallings, then the Aggies' coach. "That's why we came up with those plays we called Texas Specials."

Stallings pulled the chair from under the Longhorns in 1965 and 1966. In the first game, he had quarterback Harry Ledbetter throw what looked like a misdirected pass toward Jim Kauffman in the flat.

"We rehearsed every bit of it," Stallings said. "Ledbetter had to throw the ball into the ground and turn around disgusted. Kauffman had to angrily kick the ground and start back to the huddle."

Suddenly, Kauffman picked up the ball and threw it downfield to Dude McLean. Bang! A 91-yard exploding cigar. It wasn't an incomplete pass Ledbetter had thrown to Kauffman, but a lateral—a live ball.

The trick not only astounded the Kyle Field crowd, but sent the Aggies into a 17–0 lead. But, as Stallings would discover in the second half and in the rematch in Austin the next year, tricks are only fleeting, rickety glimpses of success. Texas came back from that 17–0 surprise to win 21–17.

Stallings pulled Texas Special II the next year. Long, the kickoff returner, faked a handoff to Lloyd Curington, ran toward the sideline, stopped at his 15 and threw a long lateral back to Curington, who ran 74 yards before he was apprehended for the fraud. The Aggies scored and crept to within 7–6, but Texas went on to a 22–14 victory.

"Those plays were fun," Kauffman once said, "and we realized they weren't good, sound football. But when you're outmanned, as we were, you have to get any edge you can."

120

Almost 40 years earlier, in 1928, the Aggies had a play where the ball was hidden behind the flexed knee of a guard, there to be picked up by a furtive runner. A Texas player, however, spotted it, grabbed it and headed toward the goal line. A&M guard Field Scovell chased the thief and caught him a few yards short of a touchdown. "A lot of good that did," Scovell later remarked. "We lost anyway 19–0."

Hargett's classy game in A&M's 1967 triumph erased the nightmares of the backfires and the long Texas winning streaks. But he soon discovered that in this rivalry a man can be standing with his cleats on the other team's neck one year and have them shoved down his throat the next year.

When Hargett met the Longhorns at the end of the 1968 season, he had thrown 176 passes without an interception. Texas intercepted him five times en route to a 35–14 victory.

In 1975, the Longhorns took the nation's top offense into Kyle Field—and lost 20–10. The Texas quarterback, Marty Akins, was on the sideline most of the afternoon with an injury.

In 1995, Texas broke a 31-game Aggie home winning streak and captured the final Southwest Conference championship with a 16–6 win at Kyle Field. Longhorn true freshman Ricky Williams churned for 163 of his team's 246 rushing yards against an A&M defense that had been allowing just 91.8 yards per game on the ground.

The 1998 Texas-Texas A&M game provided the backdrop for one of the most memorable events in college football history. It wasn't that the Aggies fought back from 23–7 down to take a 24–23 lead. It wasn't that unranked Texas finally prevailed over the sixth-ranked Aggies 26–24 on a game-winning field goal by Kris Stockton with seconds remaining in the game. It wasn't even that Williams broke Tony Dorsett's 22-year old NCAA career rushing record. It was how he did it—on a scintillating 60-yard jaunt through the nation's second-ranked defense.

The 1983 matchup was one of the biggest double-barreled surprises in the history of Kyle Field, one of those games so shattered by unreal events that it can't be put back together in a logical explanation.

Texas was 10–0. The Aggies were 5–4–1 and hoping to fire one last shocking shot at the end of the season—and they almost did, taking a 13–0 lead in the second period. That was hard enough to believe. Much harder to comprehend was the Longhorns' comeback. Riding the arm of quarterback Rick McIvor, they scored 45 points in a 15-minute blitzkrieg and won 45–13.

But for sheer strangeness, it's hard to top the 2004 game. The Longhorns had driven 88 yards to the Aggie 1 with less than 30 seconds remaining in the first half. Texas quarterback Vince Young stretched the ball out with his right hand in an attempt to break the plane of the goal line when A&M linebacker Justin Warren punched the ball out of Young's hand. Aggie cornerback Jonte Buhl scooped up the ball and sprinted 98 yards for a touchdown, giving the Aggies a 13–6 halftime lead.

Early in the third quarter, UT safety Michael Griffin blocked an Aggie punt, which Bobby Tatum recovered for a touchdown. Backup quarterback Matt Nordgren, subbing for injured regular holder Tony Jeffery, dropped the snap on the PAT attempt, initiating a chaotic botch that ended with Texas A&M's Jaxson Appel on top of the ball in the end zone for—get this—a 1-point safety, tying the game at 13. The Longhorns took command of the game from there and won 26–13. Heading into 2005, they have not lost to the Aggies yet in this century.

QB Randy McEachern

TALKIN' TEXAS FOOTBALL

We thought we'd go straight to the source and let some of Texas' greatest legends share their thoughts about Longhorn football. They put it much better than we could.

"*I never went bear-huntin' with a switch.*" DARRELL K. ROYAL, ON HIS HABIT OF RECRUITING GREAT PLAYERS TO PLAY AT TEXAS

"I'm not a football fan, but I am a fan of people, and I am a *Darrell Royal fan because he is the rarest of human beings."* FORMER PRESIDENT LYNDON JOHNSON

"When I got ready for Arkansas, I was like the players. *We were p— off, and we stayed that way until the game was over. It's just a frame of mind. You know, the leaves up there turn earlier in the fall. We'd be on the bus, and I'd notice the leaves, or see a Hog bumper sticker, and get p— off. I had on my gameface."* DARRELL K. ROYAL, ON THE RIVALRY WITH ARKANSAS (ATHLON SOUTHWEST FOOTBALL, 1979)

"Earl Campbell is the secret.
Coaches who have an Earl Campbell know
the secret. Those who don't have an Earl
Campbell, don't." Darrell K. Royal, on
the impetus behind Texas' undefeated
1977 regular season

"*And now, the moment we've been waiting for:* the award for the most outstanding college football player in America goes to Earl Campbell." THE FIRST HEISMAN WINNER, JAY BERWANGER, AT THE DOWNTOWN ATHLETIC CLUB'S HEISMAN TROPHY AWARD CEREMONY, 1977

"Mack Brown's like the Darrell Royal of the 21st century. *He's hardworking and has great concern for his athletes. The coaches and players work hard and support one another, and that's exactly how Coach Royal ran things."* JERRY SISEMORE, TEXAS ALL-AMERICAN AND ALL-PRO OFFENSIVE TACKLE

"I grew up in Southern California, and it was a little unorthodox to go all the way to Texas for school. People would always ask me, 'Why did you go there?' I would tell any kid, depending on what you want and what you value, go to the school that fits you best. I say if you want to play for a good football team, play for a great coach, win a lot of games and have a great time, go to the University of Texas."

HEISMAN TROPHY WINNER RICKY WILLIAMS

"Honestly, I don't think there's anything better in this world than being an athlete at the University of Texas." RECORD-SETTING LONGHORN QB CHRIS SIMMS

"I'm looking forward to being out there in my Texas jersey with all of the guys for one more year." RUNNING BACK CEDRIC BENSON, ANNOUNCING THAT HE WOULD RETURN FOR HIS SENIOR SEASON

"*We want our linemen to run like our linebackers.* We want our linebackers to run like our DBs and wide receivers. And we want our running backs, wide receivers and DBs to run like the fastest men in the world." TEXAS STRENGTH COACH JEFF "MAD DOG" MADDEN

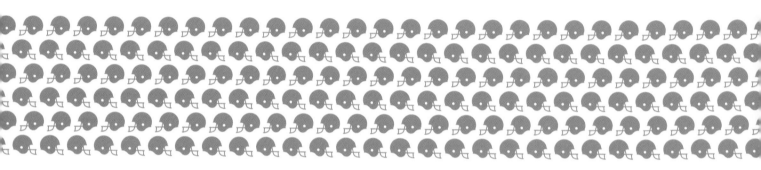

"*On game days at Texas, you get a fresh new sense of Texas pride* throughout the stadium when they give the Hook 'em Horns sign and sing 'The Eyes of Texas.' Coach Brown has established the true spirit of wearing the burnt orange and white together. The team, the faculty, the students, the alumni and the community are united together as family—and that's becoming a strong force again in Austin." LONGHORN GREAT TOMMY NOBIS

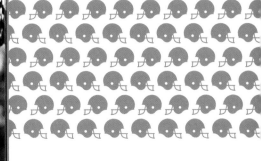

"You've never played in an all-out, fight-for-your-life, back-yard-brawl rivalry until you've played in a Texas-Texas A&M game. It's an experience you will never forget." TEXAS ALL-BIG 12 DEFENSIVE LINEMAN SHAUN ROGERS

"The feeling you get when you hear 'The Eyes of Texas' after a win is the best feeling you could ever have." ALL-AMERICA RECEIVER ROY WILLIAMS

"I'm still burning orange." PRIEST HOLMES, TEXAS RUNNING BACK AND NFL ALL-PRO

"You can't help but stand up and put up the Horns sign when they play 'The Eyes of Texas.' It takes you over. Whether you're in Orlando, Columbus, Detroit, Ann Arbor or wherever, you stand up and it gets into your heart and soul." ESPN's LEE CORSO

"I'm ready to go to Dallas and stick my chest out and bump into as many OU folks as I can this October. With our big boys up front, this is our year. It's time for Mack Brown to start a streak of his own." KENNETH SIMS, 1981 LOMBARDI TROPHY WINNER AND TOP PICK IN THE 1982 NFL DRAFT (DALLAS MORNING NEWS)

FACTS AND FIGURES
Texas Bowl Game Scores

RECORD: 21-21-2			
DATE	BOWL	OPPONENT	RESULT
Jan. 1, 1943	Cotton	Georgia Tech	W 14–7
Jan. 1, 1944	Cotton	Randolph Field	T 7–7
Jan. 1, 1946	Cotton	Missouri	W 40–27
Jan. 1, 1948	Sugar	Alabama	W 27–7
Jan. 1, 1949	Orange	Georgia	W 41–28
Jan. 1, 1951	Cotton	Tennessee	L 20–14
Jan. 1, 1953	Cotton	Tennessee	W 16–0
Jan. 1, 1958	Sugar	Ole Miss	L 39–7
Jan. 1, 1960	Cotton	Syracuse	L 23–14
Dec. 17, 1960	Bluebonnet	Alabama	T 3–3
Jan. 1, 1962	Cotton	Ole Miss	W 12–7
Jan. 1, 1963	Cotton	LSU	L 13–0
Jan. 1, 1964	Cotton	Navy	W 28–6
Jan. 1, 1965	Orange	Alabama	W 21–17
Dec. 17, 1966	Bluebonnet	Ole Miss	W 19–0
Jan. 1, 1969	Cotton	Tennessee	W 36–13
Jan. 1, 1970	Cotton	Notre Dame	W 21–17
Jan. 1, 1971	Cotton	Notre Dame	L 24–11
Jan. 1, 1972	Cotton	Penn State	L 30–6

RECORD: 21-21-2

DATE	BOWL	OPPONENT	RESULT
Jan. 1, 1973	Cotton	Alabama	W 17–13
Jan. 1, 1974	Cotton	Nebraska	L 19–3
Dec. 30, 1974	Gator	Auburn	L 27–3
Dec. 27, 1975	Bluebonnet	Colorado	W 38–21
Jan. 1, 1978	Cotton	Notre Dame	L 38–10
Dec. 23, 1978	Sun	Maryland	W 42–0
Dec. 22, 1979	Sun	Washington	L 14–7
Dec. 31, 1980	Bluebonnet	North Carolina	L 16–7
Jan. 1, 1982	Cotton	Alabama	W 14–12
Dec. 25, 1982	Sun	North Carolina	L 26–10
Jan. 2, 1984	Cotton	Georgia	L 10–9
Dec. 26, 1984	Freedom	Iowa	L 55–17
Dec. 31, 1985	Bluebonnet	Air Force	L 24–16
Dec. 31, 1987	Bluebonnet	Pittsburgh	W 32–27
Jan. 1, 1991	Cotton	Miami	L 46–3
Dec. 30, 1994	Sun	North Carolina	W 35–31
Dec. 31, 1995	Sugar	Virginia Tech	L 28–10
Jan. 1, 1997	Fiesta	Penn State	L 38–15
Jan. 1, 1999	Cotton	Mississippi State	W 38–11
Jan. 1, 2000	Cotton	Arkansas	L 27–6
Dec. 29, 2000	Holiday	Oregon	L 35–30
Dec. 28, 2001	Holiday	Washington	W 47–43
Jan. 1, 2003	Cotton	LSU	W 35–20
Dec. 30, 2003	Holiday	Washington State	L 28–20
Jan. 1, 2005	Rose	Michigan	W 38–37

Career Statistical Leaders

Rushes: 1,112, Cedric Benson, 2001-04

Rushing Yards: 6,279, Ricky Williams, 1995-98

Rushing Yards per Game: 136.5, Ricky Williams, 1995-98

Rushing Touchdowns: 72, Ricky Williams, 1995-98

Pass Attempts: 1,065, Major Applewhite, 1998-2001

Pass Completions: 611, Major Applewhite, 1998-2001

Passing Yards: 8,353, Major Applewhite, 1998-2001

Passing Touchdowns: 60, Major Applewhite, 1998-2001

Receptions: 241, Roy Williams, 2000-03

Receiving Yards: 3,866, Roy Williams, 1000-03

Touchdown Receptions: 36, Roy Williams, 2000-03

Total Offense Yards: 8,059, Major Applewhite, 1998-2001

Points Scored: 452, Ricky Williams, 1995-98

Punt Return Average (Min. 25): 17.7 yards, Bobby Dillon, 1949-51

Kickoff Return Average (Min. 12): 29.1 yards, Phil Harris, 1963-65

Total Tackles: 499, Britt Hager, 1984-88

Sacks: 40.5, Kiki DeAyala, 1979-82

Interceptions: 17, Nathan Vasher, 2000-03, and Noble Doss, 1939-41

Longhorns in the Pros

Rod Babers	DB	Tampa Bay Buccaneers
Cedric Benson	RB	Chicago Bears
Leonard Davis	T	Arizona Cardinals
Phil Dawson	K	Cleveland Browns
Derrick Dockery	G	Washington Redskins
Casey Hampton	DT	Pittsburgh Steelers
Priest Holmes	RB	Kansas City Chiefs
Quentin Jammer	DB	San Diego Chargers
B.J. Johnson	WR	Denver Broncos
Derrick Johnson	LB	Kansas City Chiefs
D.D. Lewis	LB	Seattle Seahawks
Cullen Loeffler	C	Minnesota Vikings
Will Matthews	FB	Detroit Lions
Dam Neil	G	Denver Broncos
Cory Redding	DE	Detroit Lions
Shaun Rogers	DT	Detroit Lions
Bo Scaife	TE	Tennessee Titans
Chris Simms	QB	Tampa Bay Buccaneers
Sloan Thomas	WR	Houston Texans
Kalen Thornton	LB	Dallas Cowboys
Marcus Tubbs	DT	Seattle Seahawks
Nathan Vasher	DB	Chicago Bears
Marcus Wilkins	LB	Cincinnati Bengals
Mike Williams	T	Buffalo Bills
Roy Williams	WR	Detroit Lions
Cedric Woodard	DE	Seattle Seahawks

First-Round Draft Picks

2005	RB Cedric Benson, Chicago Bears
	LB Derrick Johnson, Kansas City Chiefs
2004	DT Marcus Tubbs, Seattle Seahawks
	WR Roy Williams, Detroit Lions
2002	CB Quentin Jammer, San Diego Chargers
	T Mike Williams, Buffalo Bills
2001	T Leonard Davis, Arizona Cardinals
	DT Casey Hampton, Pittsburgh Steelers
1999	RB Ricky Williams, New Orleans Saints
1997	CB Bryant Westbrook, Detroit Lions
1995	T Blake Brockermeyer, Carolina Panthers
1991	S Stanley Richard, San Diego Chargers
	T Stan Thomas, Chicago Bears
1989	RB Eric Metcalf, Cleveland Browns
1985	CB Jerry Gray, Los Angeles Rams
1984	CB Mossy Cade, San Diego Chargers
1982	DE Kenneth Sims, New England Patriots
1980	WR Johnny "Lam" Jones, New York Jets
	DB Johnnie Johnson, Los Angeles Rams
	DB Derrick Hatchett, Baltimore Colts

1979	PK Russell Erxleben, New Orleans Saints
1978	RB Earl Campbell, Houston Oilers
1977	DB Raymond Clayborn, New England Patriots
1973	T Jerry Sisemore, Philadelphia Eagles
1970	T Bob McKay, Cleveland Browns
1966	LB Tommy Nobis, Atlanta Falcons
1964	T Scott Appleton, Dallas Cowboys
1956	E Menan Schriewer, Chicago Bears
1953	E Tom Stolhanske, San Francisco 49ers
	G Harley Sewell, Detroit Lions
1951	G Bud McFadin, Los Angeles Rams
1949	C Dick Harris, Chicago Bears
1948	QB Bobby Layne, Chicago Bears
	E Max Bumgardner, Chicago Bears
1947	E Hub Bechtol, Pittsburgh Steelers
1942	RB Orban "Spec" Sanders, Washington Redskins